Acknowledging the efforts of all the members of Inner Whcel Club Shimla

Dear Friends,

It's an amazing effort to attempt to upload an e book on home remedies for simple problems in everyday life. Digitalisation of these solutions will reach countless persons specially youth of today who prefer to read on their phones rather than in print. Simple household solutions to the problems which stare at us in our daily life and are slowly becoming extinct will reach out to a generation which finds it easy to read them on Internet.

My heartiest congratulations to President Shalini Dhadwal of Inner Wheel Club of Shimla in her attempt to make the youth of today aware of these dying remedies. May the solutions to day to day problems reach out to and benefit scores of people. My best wishes.

Regards.

Yours in Inner Wheel
Renu Baljee
Past IIW Board Director

Dear Shalini

I am so happy to know that you are planning to publish a book on
'Dadi ma ke Nuskhey' This is a very much need of the modern times and
an innovative way to do good for our members as well as the community
It can help in providing remedies with no side effects and also affordable
I am sure, this book will benefit all sections of society and remind us of
our forgotten treasures. My congratulations and best wishes for your new
endeavor

Your 's - in Friendship
Kanan Diwan
PDC

Dear Shalini,

Why we must know about Dadi, Nani's Nuskhe? There are many useful and beneficial traditional recipes which are healthy and also beauty secrets.
Today we are in the rat race of the marketing strategy of commercial ads on TV and follow them blindly after spending a lot of money. We have no time to sit with our Nani / Dadi or even with mother to learn our traditional Nuskhas , which can be made out of ingredients available in our Kitchen/ home. I advise the young generation to spend some time with their Nani/ Dadi and learn from them their useful Nuskhas before it goes with them.

I am glad to know that you have compiled a book "Dadi Ke Nushkey" which will go a long way to create awareness among our members.
I wish great success for your Noble work.

Lots of love & regards,
Meena Ranaut
P.D.C

Dear Friends,

I would like to extend my heartiest congratulations to the President Shalini Dhadwal and her team of Inner Wheel Shimla for publishing this interesting book. In this day and age when everything is only instant this book brings back the wholesome gems from yesteryears which are nearly lost. Congratulations again for the wonderful effort .

Yours Sincerely,
Bhuvan Rana
PDC

Dear Shalini

It is a matter of great pride that you are bringing out an EBOOK on Dadi ma ke Nuske . Ever thankful to you for giving me an opportunity to be part of the book . I am sure with your diligence, hard work & perfection the book will be of great value to one & all .We all remember our childhood days when our mother & grandmother referred to these home remedies before running to the doctor. This book will be one of your land mark project. Congratulations once again for this brilliant idea .

Wishing you all the best .
Neelam Vij
PDC

Dear Readers,

Growing up in a traditional Indian family exposed me to many home-made remedies.These remedies were not only cost effective but also without side effects. Upon becoming President of Innerwheel Club of Shimla for the term 2023-24, I thought of making   some of these remedies known to others too. My team mates especially Meenakshi Kuthiala, PDC Neelam Vij and Nirupama Chaudhry helped me in achieving this task. Last but not the least I want to thank Siddharth Kuthiala and my daughter Muskaan Dhadwal for the technical help. I hope this book benefits many.

Love and regards,

Dr Shalini Dhadwal
President
IWC Shimla
2023-24

EXECUTIVE TEAM 2023 - 2024

Mrs. Reetika Lal
Vice President

Mrs. Renu Butail
Secretary

Mrs.Umang Banga
Joint Secretary

Mrs.Sonal Aggarwal
Treasurer

Mrs. Namita Nag
ISO

Mrs. Sonia Arora
Editor

IPP Dr. Alka Sharma Kaushal

PP Mrs. Madhu Sood

Mrs.Meenakshi Kuthiala

Mrs. Rajani Verma

Mrs. Geetu Kukreja

Mrs. Abbu Arora

Nosebleed

- **Immediate treatment for stopping nosebleed**: Dissolve three grams of alum in water and apply the solution to both nostrils. The nosebleed will stop immediately.
- **Auxiliary treatment**: Pour cold water over the head to stop bleeding from the nose.

Dental problems remedy

- **For dental diseases**: Crush rock salt finely like flour, sieve it, mix it with two grams of mustard oil (four times the quantity of salt), and massage the gums with it. After massaging for a while, rinse with lukewarm water. This method will relieve the sour, hot, and cold sensation in teeth, and the teeth will become strong.

Bad breath

- **Bad breath**: Keep a clove in your mouth and suck on it after every meal to get rid of bad breath and foul-smelling breath.

Mouth ulcers

- **Small mouth ulcers:** Apply finely powdered harad (hartaki) on the ulcers to heal them and get relief from mouth ulcers.

Disturbed taste in the mouth

- **Correcting bad taste in the mouth**: Cut a lemon, add two pinches of black salt and ground black pepper to one half, heat it slightly on low heat or place it on a hotplate. Sucking on this mixture will alleviate the bitterness in the mouth.

Night cough and phlegm disorder

- **Coughing at night and phlegm disorder**: Keep a piece of betel nut and a piece of peeled ginger in the mouth and keep sucking on them to relieve coughing and facilitate easy phlegm removal, providing relief from ticklish cough and aiding better sleep.

Throat irritation

- **Throat irritation**: Gargle with a mixture of warm water and a tablespoon of warm water a few times a day to relieve throat irritation.

Throat swelling and pain

- **Throat swelling and pain**: Dissolve alum in warm water and gargle with it two to three times. If this is not possible, gargle with half a teaspoon of salt in a glass of warm water, which will also be beneficial.

Acidity

- **Acidity**: Chewing one clove in the morning and evening after meals helps in acidity relief and is beneficial in all acidity-related diseases. Clove powder equivalent to two grams mixed with jaggery and consumed with water helps in acidity relief. It should be consumed for three consecutive days after dinner, which cures acidity.

Immediate relief from pain

- **For immediate relief**: Peel and wrap a clove of garlic in a raisin. Chew and swallow it after meals, which will expel the trapped air from the stomach and also relieve back pain caused by cold.

Loss of appetite and weakness

- Loss of appetite and weakness: Peel and finely chop one to three grams of ginger, sprinkle a little rock salt, and eat it once a day for eight days before meals. This will improve digestion, increase appetite, and clear stomach gas.

Constipation:

- Drinking the juice of two oranges every morning for eight to ten consecutive days can help alleviate constipation. Avoid consuming spices, salt, or ice immediately after drinking the juice. Refrain from eating anything for one to two hours after consuming the juice. Avoid habits such as consuming flour-based or fried items, highly spiced foods, alcohol, coffee, tea, meat, fish, late-night meals, drinking water from the freezer immediately after meals, and sitting for prolonged periods at night, etc.

Harmless piles:

- Taking one to five teaspoons of castor oil mixed with one cup of warm water or milk before going to bed helps relieve constipation. For adults, usually, two to four teaspoons are sufficient. Individuals with severe constipation may take up to eight teaspoons of castor oil, while others may find relief with just thirty drops.

Hiccup:

- Grind 5 grams of cloves and 10 grams of sugar candy into a fine powder, then mix it with 30 grams of water and drink it to alleviate hiccups and indigestion.
- Take four small cardamoms, peel them, crush them, and boil them in 500 grams of water. Once 200 grams of water remains, strain it and give it to the patient to drink. This remedy helps stop hiccups instantly.

Nausea and vomiting:

- Mix 3 grams of cumin and 6 grams of sugar candy to make a powder. Ingesting this powder with water helps alleviate vomiting, bleeding, nausea, and loss of appetite. Take it two to three times a day as needed.

Severe vomiting:

- When experiencing vomiting due to medication, dissolve one teaspoon of lime water in 125 grams of milk and drink it twice a day. This helps alleviate fever-induced vomiting and yellow fever.

Navel pain:

- Mix 20 grams of fennel seeds with an equal amount of jaggery and consume it empty stomach in the morning. It helps relieve displaced navel pain.

Kidney pain:

- Take dried basil leaves, 20 grams, dry ajwain (carom seeds), 20 grams, and rock salt, 10 grams, grind them into a powder, and take two grams of this powder with warm water twice a day to alleviate kidney pain. It's effective for coughs and colds.

Burning sensation in the urinary bladder:

- Mix thickly ground coriander seeds with jaggery in equal amounts and consume it. It helps alleviate the burning sensation in the urinary bladder.

Piles:

- Soak two dried figs in water overnight and consume them on an empty stomach in the morning. Repeat this process in the evening between four and five o'clock.
- Avoid consuming anything for one hour before or after. Consuming buttermilk after noon is optimal. Mixing half a teaspoon of ground carom seeds and one gram of rock salt in buttermilk after lunch benefits piles

Prevention of nasal congestion and cold:

- In the night, sniffing a few drops of warm mustard oil or cow ghee through the nose prevents nasal congestion. It keeps the brain healthy and prevents nasal diseases.

Prevention of dry lips:

- Applying mustard oil in the navel daily prevents chapped lips and makes them soft and beautiful. It also relieves itching and dryness of the eyes.

For strong teeth:

- Rubbing the gums with fingertips while passing stool and urine daily prevents tooth decay. It also eliminates the fear of stroke, pyorrhea, bleeding from the teeth, and tooth movement.

For pimples, moles, and pimples:

- Applying a few drops of castor oil on pimples every morning helps clear them within a month or two. Additionally, massaging the face or body with castor oil two to three times a day gradually eliminates moles, blemishes, brown spots, pimples, or small pimples on the cheeks or skin.

Amhoriya:

- If there are fine pimples or blisters on your face or back due to heat and humidity, squeezing a lemon into a glass of water and drinking it twice a day will quickly cure amhoriya.

For nail beauty:

- If your nails are rough and weak, applying lemon juice on a cotton pad or rubbing lemon peel and then washing your hands after a while regularly for a few days will create a natural shine on the nails and make them stronger.

Quitting alcohol addiction:

- Drinking apple juice repeatedly and eating apples with meals helps overcome the habit of alcohol consumption, and develops aversion to every intoxicating substance.

For quitting tea addiction:

- After boiling a clove, two black peppers, and four basil leaves in a cup of water, adding some milk and sugar to it, and drinking it with tea two to three times a day can help break the habit of tea addiction.

Stuttering:

- Boil 5 grams of fennel in 300 grams of water. When the water is reduced to 100 grams, add 50 grams of sugar and 250 grams of cow's milk. Drink it before bed every day, and within a few days, stuttering will be corrected.

Black cough:

- Mixing roasted alum and two grains of sugar together and taking it twice a day helps cure black cough within five days, giving double the dose to adults. If unable to take without water, give a sip of hot water.

If milk is not digestible for children:
- While boiling milk, add a gram of small peepal (pippli) to 200 grams of milk. After boiling the milk, strain it and discard the peepal before drinking. This peepal removes the impurities present in the milk and makes it digestible.

For stuttering and stammering:
- If a child chews a fresh green amla daily for a few days, stuttering and stammering disappear. The tongue becomes thin, and the voice becomes clear. The heat of the mouth also subsides.

For beautiful offspring:
- Feeding two oranges at noon daily to a pregnant woman from the first month to the eighth month makes the child beautiful with a good complexion.

Eczema:
- Take 250 grams of mustard oil and boil it in an iron pan. When the oil starts boiling well, add 50 grams of neem copal. Remove the pan from the fire as soon as the copal turns black; otherwise, the copal can burn in the oil. After cooling, strain the oil and fill it in a bottle. Apply it to eczema two to three times a day. Eczema will be cured in a few days. If applied for a year, this disease will not recur.

For bleeding from cuts:
- If blood flows from a cut with a blade or knife, applying cotton soaked in real turpentine oil to the cut area stops the blood flow within a short time. If a blade or knife gets stuck, tying a bandage soaked in one's urine will stop the bleeding, and the wound will heal quickly.

If hair gets stuck in the stomach or throat:
- Eating finely chopped pieces of pineapple peel with black pepper and rock salt makes the hair, thorn, or glass disappear in the stomach.

If cucumber or glass gets stuck in the throat:
- Soak three tablespoons of isabgol husk in a glass of cold water. After soaking, add borax as needed and drink it. If a thorn gets stuck in a child's foot and does not come out, melt jaggery on the fire and mix finely crushed ajwain in it. Apply it lukewarm to the place. The thorn will come out on its own.

For joint pain:
- Drinking the juice of fresh fenugreek leaves fifteen grams daily eliminates arthritis. Do not add salt, sugar, etc., to this juice. Take it empty stomach or at four in the evening. Take it for a month or two. Knead the dough, add fenugreek leaves, make chapattis, and eat them once a day. This will provide quick relief.

To reduce obesity:
- Boil 125 grams of water and cool it. When it becomes lukewarm, add 15 grams of lemon juice and 15 grams of honey. Drink it like a syrup.

For back pain:
- Soak six grams of fenugreek seeds in water overnight. In the morning, grind these soaked fenugreek seeds with poppy seeds and thirty grams of coriander. Make a fine paste and cook it. Make a porridge and eat it once a day as required for a week or two.

For knee pain:
- Applying a poultice of fenugreek leaves mixed with water twice a day relieves knee pain. Especially in old age, knees do not hurt. This also relieves heel pain. Take it for a month or two continuously.

For headache:
- Applying two to four drops of fresh cow ghee through the nose in the morning and evening, or sniffing it regularly, relieves the pain of migraine from the root. Additionally, bleeding from the nose is also eliminated from the root. Take it for seven days.

KITCHEN TIPS AND TRICKS
- If you happen to over-salt a pot of soup, just drop in a peeled potato. The potato will absorb the excess salt.
- When boiling eggs, add a pinch of salt to keep the shells from cracking.
- Never put citrus fruits(Oranges, Lemons, limes, etc) or tomatoes in the fridge. The low temperatures degrade the aroma and flavor of these fruits. (That's why our tomatoes don't last in the fridge)
- To clean iron cook-ware, don't use detergents. Just scrub them with salt and a clean, dry paper towel.
- When storing empty airtight containers, throw in a pinch of salt to keep them from getting stinky.
- If you are making gravy(stew) and accidentally burn it, just pour it into a clean pan and continue cooking it. Add sugar a little at a time, tasting as you go to avoid 'over-sugaring' it. The sugar will cancel out the burned taste.
- Burned a pot of rice? Just place a piece of white bread on top of the rice for 5-10 minutes to draw out the burned flavor. Be careful not to scrape the burned pieces off of the bottom of the pan when serving the rice.

Astringent lotion:

- To make your own astringent lotion blanch a small peach, remove its stone and grind and squeeze out its juice. Add to it one-fourth teaspoon each of lime and tomato juice. Mix well and spread over your entire face and neck and leave it on for about 10 to 15 minutes. This serves as a very good astringent.

Apple tonic:

- Peel and grate a small apple. Squeeze out its juice and stir in a few drops of lime juice. Spread the lotion on your face and neck and leave it on for 15 minutes. Wash off with lukewarm water then splash on cold water. It is an excellent tonic for counteracting a greasy skin.

Amla lotion:

- To 4 tablespoons of fresh amla juice add equal quantity of strained lime juice. Mix well and rub into the hair roots two hours before going in for your head bath. This lotion helps the hair to grow long, thick and lustrous.

All-purpose cream:

- Take 1 teaspoon each of rice flour, jowar, gram and wheat flour. Mix them together and set aside. Now take 1 small piece of multani mitti and soak it in a little water until it turns soft. Add the flours along with enough cream to form a thick cream. Apply the cream thickly on the face and neck. Leave it on until it starts feeling a little dry, then start rubbing your face slowly but with vigour with your hands. The paste will go on falling as you will keep on rubbing your face.

Moisturizing cream:

- Soak 4 almonds, 8 charolis, 1 walnut meat in milk overnight. Next morning, grind the nuts to a fine paste in milk. Stir in 3 tablespoons of cream of milk, 4 tablespoons of cucumber juice and a few drops of essence of rose. Mix well and put the cream in a small bottle and set it either in the fridge or a cool, dark and a dry place. Apply this cream every morning over your entire face and neck. Wash it off one hour after its application first with hot and then with cold water. This cream will counteract any tendency to wrinkles and dryness and give your complexion a flower-like bloom.

Kaajal:

- Fill a clean sterilized copper, steel or silver diya with pure ghee or mustard oil. Make a wick from sterilized cotton and soak it in oil. Light the wick. Hang or place a small pot one-fourth of an inch away from the burning wick. When the oil has been exhausted in the diya, remove the pot and you will find soot on its surface. Mix this well with a little castor oil and store this kaajal in a clean box. It is excellent for keeping the eyes sparkling.

Hair removing cream:
- Take 1 kilo of cleaned masoor dal and soak it in coconut juice. Keep it in the sun until it turns dry thoroughly, then break 2 eggs in it and mix thoroughly into the dal. Set the dal once again in the burning sun until it turns dry completely. Then have it ground to a fine powder from the flour mill. Store this powder in an airtight box or tin. Every morning, take a tablespoon of this flour and add enough water or milk to make it into a thick and smooth paste. Mix it thoroughly and apply on any portion of your body where you have a thin growth of hair like face, arms etc. Leave it on until it turns quite dry, then rub your face with your hands slowly but with vigour. The paste will go on falling as you will keep on rubbing your face. Remove the paste which still clings on with lukewarm water and then with cold. This cream not only decreases the growth of hair considerably if used regularly, but at the same time also frees the skin of all its embarrassing blemishes.

Hand cream:
- Take a tablespoon of olive oil and add enough salt to form a thick paste. Work this cream into your hands with the same movements as in

Piles and Asthma:
- In a bottle of Vaseline put about twelve drops of Amritdhara. Mix the Vaseline thoroughly with a spoon. Before passing your stools every morning, just apply the medicine with a piece of cotton wool to the piles. For a few days, you will feel a burning sensation that will keep you uncomfortable for a few minutes every morning, but within a couple of days your piles will burn away and you feel relieved and on top of the world once again. If you use this treatment regularly, you will not be put to the inconvenience of an operation table.
- Another remedy for piles is to mix five tolas of fresh onion juice with one tola of ground sugar candy, take twice daily, and drink water over it. If your piles bleed then take curd and mix in freshly ground onion and ground sugar candy to suit the taste. Eat this regularly until you are cured.
- The best remedy for Asthma is to take 250 grams each of fresh onion juice and pure honey and mix in one chatak of soda bicarbonate. Mix well and give one teaspoon of this mixture to the patient both morning and evening.

Weak Memory and Dizziness:
- If you have a weak memory take every night before going to bed one cup of carrot juice mixed with one cup of milk and honey to suit the taste, and follow this with ten almonds.
- If you are suffering from regular spells of dizziness, then take half a cup of flour, 4 to 6 peppercorns, one-fourth teaspoon of cumin seeds, one-fourth cup of sugar, three cups milk, 25 grams each of almonds, pistachios, and walnuts, and half teaspoon cardamom seeds. Grind the sugar and add to the flour along with peppercorns, cumin seeds, and enough water to form a batter of medium consistency. Grind together all the nuts and cardamom seeds. Heat the milk, add sugar to taste and nuts, and cook

stirring all the time until the milk is reduced to half the original quantity Remove from fire and keep it warm. Now heat enough pure ghee for deep frying. When blue smoke rises from the surface of the ghee, drop a tablespoon of the batter in it and spread it into a thin round shape. Deep fry gently to a golden brown color. Drain thoroughly and put three malpuras into the prepared mix. You can consume the mix regularly and within a few weeks you'll get rid of the dizziness.

Deep Dark Circles Under the Eyes:
- Deep, dark circles under the eyes not only spoil the facial charm but at the same time add years to your age. To avoid them, take plenty of fresh green and yellow vegetables and fruits, especially citrus fruits, and only balanced amounts of proteins and starch. Besides taking a diet rich in fruits and vegetables, avoid reading late at night or keeping late nights and long hours of work which require close visual concentration like sewing, writing, and reading.

- Always keep to the golden rule of early to bed and early to rise.
- If your work requires close visual concentration give yourself a break from time to time.
- Close your eyes. Cover them with the palms of your hands and forgetting the world.

Anti-wrinkle cream:
- Take 1 egg white, beat it nicely, and add to it an equal quantity of honey. Add enough flour to form a thick and smooth paste. Now clean the face with a cleansing lotion and then steam your face for about 10 minutes. Pat on cold cream in a thick layer on your face and on top apply the honey paste nicely in a thick layer. After fifteen minutes remove the cream with a napkin squeezed out in warm water. Then splash on some cold water to close the pores. This cream should be used once every week by all women above the age of twenty-five if you want your skin to remain wrinkle-free, soft, and smooth. This is a cream which is used widely by most of the actresses abroad.

Anti-pimple cream:
- Blanch eight almonds and grind them to a paste with a fresh and sweet-smelling Rose. Stir in one-fourth teaspoon of glycerine, 1 small piece of camphor, and a few drops of essence of rose. Apply this cream every day for one hour before going in for your bath if you are a victim of pimples. This cream not only helps in combating pimples but at the same time clears the skin of all its blemishes.

Cucumber tonic:
- Grind a small tender cucumber and squeeze out its juice. Stir in an equal quantity of milk. This is an excellent whitening tonic for delicate skin.

Cleansing lotion:
- To 1 tablespoon of milk add a few drops of lime juice, apply on your entire face and neck, and leave on for five minutes. Wipe off with a piece of cotton wool. This is a good cleansing lotion for greasy skin.

Cleansing cream:
- To a tablespoon of gram flour add enough water to make it into a thick and smooth paste. Put in 1 teaspoon of cream of milk and a few drops of lime juice. Mix it thoroughly and apply it with your

fingertips over your entire face and neck. Leave it on for a minute, then remove it like all-purpose cream. This cream cleanses and purifies the pores of your skin so that they may function in the way nature intended them to.

Whitening lotion:
- To one tablespoon of cucumber juice add one-fourth teaspoon of lime juice and a pinch of turmeric powder. Mix well and apply over your face and neck. Leave it on for half an hour, then remove it with ordinary tap water. This lotion makes an excellent whitener for all types of skin

Patches on the Skin:
- Patches are either dark or light in color. The light ones can be cured by either rubbing a little mustard oil vigorously onto the patch or rubbing tulsi or ribbed geird leaf onto the patch once or twice daily. Dark patches can be eased away by rubbing either cucumber, tomato, or lime juice onto the patches.

Women's Diseases:
- Many women are troubled by too much bleeding during menopause. To control this bleeding take the skin of a very red pomegranate and dry the skin nicely. in the sun. Preserve it in an airtight container. Break a small piece of the skin and fry it to a golden brown colour in pure ghee, then pound it to a fine powder. Put the powder in a spoon and fill it up with sugar. Eat the mixture and drink water over it immediately. Over this, eat wheat halwa made with pure ghee. Take this treatment from the day the menses start to the third day only for effective results.
- Too much menstrual bleeding in young women can be controlled by eating moong dal halwa. To prepare the halwa take 1 table- spoon whole moong with skins. 3 tbsps. pure ghee. 2 tbsps. each of finely sliced almonds and, pistachios. 2 tsp. cardamom seeds and sugar to taste.
- Pound dal to a fine powder. Heat ghee and fry the grounded dal to a golden brown colour. Add the rest of the ingredients and cook stirring frequently until the ghee floats on the top. Take this halwa from the day the menses start to the third day for three months and you will be relieved of your trouble for good.
- If you are one of those who always gets late menses, then eat raw onion with food regularly and you will always get menses on time. The best treatment for Leukorrhea (white vaginal discharge) is to take one teaspoon of fresh onion juice with half a teaspoon of honey twice. daily until you are cured of your malady.

Diabetes and Pain in the Joints:
- The best remedy for diabetes and painful joints is bitter-gourd tea. Cut unpeeled bitter gourds into small pieces and place them in a bowl. Cover them with water. Cover the bowl and set aside the whole night. Next morning strain out the water and drink about a glass of it first thing after you have brushed your teeth. Take this tea regularly for three years and you will be completely cured of these two above-mentioned diseases:

- Besides taking this tea, if you at the same time will massage your joints with medicated mustard oil you will get relief quicker. To make the oil take one bottle of pure mustard oil, one teaspoon each of mustard seeds, ajwain, cumin seeds, and peppercorns. One-inch dry ginger. One pod of garlic, 1 onion. Handful of neem piece leaves. Grind all the ingredients to a paste and add to the oil. Heat the oil to boiling, reduce heat, and cook until the paste turns dark and crisp. Then add a little camphor Boil again for a few minutes. Remove from fire Cool, strain, and bottle. Massage at least once daily

Acute Tonsils:
- For acute tonsils gargle with spinach tea to get relief. Boil spinach leaves, say about twelve in a cup of water Remove from fire, strain, and cool. Add a dash of salt and use as a gargle. Gargle at least twice daily. This is also a good remedy for sore throats

Vomiting:
- Apply salt and pepper on lime halves and heat them. Suck them slowly to get relief

For preventing scalp issues:
- Before bathing, massage your scalp with a good oil (such as coconut, mustard, sesame, brahmi-amla, or bhringraj) for about five minutes. This practice enhances memory power and keeps your hair dark, shiny, and soft.

To protect your eyes:
- After brushing your teeth in the morning, fill your mouth with water and sprinkle cold water on your eyes. Doing this three times a day (morning, noon, and evening) refreshes your eyes and prevents any eye disorders. Consistent practice may even help reduce the need for glasses.

To safeguard against dangerous and infectious diseases:
- Consume the juice of two lemons along with your meals. This helps prevent heatstroke.

To prevent heatstroke:
- During the summer season, simply carry an onion (peeled) in your pocket. This simple practice can protect you from heatstroke. Additionally, consuming raw onion with meals twice a day provides further protection.

To prevent jaundice:
- Drinking water that has been boiled and kept aside for five minutes helps prevent jaundice.

To purify contaminated water:
- Adding fresh basil leaves (around 50-60 leaves in four liters of water) to contaminated water purifies it. Strain the water through a cloth, ensuring that the basil leaves are present.

To delay aging and maintain youthfulness:

- During the amla (Indian gooseberry) season, consume two ripe amlas daily after morning exercise or a walk. If this is not feasible, dry the amlas and grind them into a powder. Before sleeping, take this powder with honey or water. Regular consumption for three to four months can transform your body. It enhances digestion, promotes deep sleep, relieves headaches, boosts virility, strengthens teeth, and keeps hair dark and beautiful, even in old age.

Inflammation in the Lungs:

- In cases of lung inflammation, which is also known as pulmonary edema, the lung tissues become swollen due to the accumulation of pathogens and immune cells. This swelling can harm the airways or lung structures. Possible causative agents for lung infections include viruses, bacteria, fungi, and parasites. Sometimes, multiple types of microorganisms may contribute to lung infections, such as when viral bronchitis transforms into bacterial pneumonia. Lung infections can occur at any age, although certain diseases are more prevalent in specific age groups. These infections can affect various parts of the respiratory system, including the bronchi, bronchioles, and alveoli. Common symptoms of lung infections include:

Excessive Mucus Production During Coughing:

- The primary function of coughing is to expel the thick mucus produced by the airways and lungs. Sometimes, this mucus may contain traces of blood.

Chest Pain Upon Breathing:

- Lung infections can cause a sharp, stabbing sensation in the chest, especially during deep breaths. Occasionally, individuals may also experience similar pain in the upper back.

Fever:

- When the body fights an infection, fever occurs. The average normal body temperature is 98.6°F (37°C), but in cases of bacterial lung infections, the fever can reach up to 105°F (40.5°C). Typically, a fever above 102°F (38.9°C) is accompanied by other symptoms, such as sweating, chills, muscle pain, and weakness.

Shortness of Breath:

- Reduced lung function due to infection can lead to difficulty in breathing. If you experience persistent shortness of breath, seek medical attention promptly.

Fatigue:

- When the body combats an infection, fatigue and weakness are common sensations. Rest and adequate sleep are essential during this time.

Wheezing Sounds:

- Wheezing or high-pitched whistling sounds during breathing may occur due to damage to the airways or swelling. These sounds are often associated with lung infections.
- If your temperature exceeds 102°F (38.9°C) or remains elevated for more than three days, consult a doctor promptly. Additionally, if you experience chest pain, difficulty breathing, or persistent cough, seek medical evaluation.

Treatment and Prevention:

- Use pain relievers like acetaminophen or ibuprofen to reduce fever.
- Stay well-hydrated by drinking plenty of water.
- Honey or ginger tea provides soothing relief.
- Gargle with warm saline water.
- Rest adequately and maintain proper humidity using a humidifier.
- Only take medications prescribed by a doctor1.

To dissolve kidney stones:

- Try the following "Ram Baan" (highly effective) remedy using horse gram (kulthi):
- Take 250 grams of horse gram and clean it thoroughly.
- Soak the horse gram in three liters of water overnight.
- The next morning, simmer the soaked horse gram (along with the water) over low heat for approximately four hours until only one liter of water remains.
- Strain the mixture and add 30 to 50 grams of desi ghee (clarified butter) according to your digestive capacity.
- You now have a stone-dissolving potion that can be consumed as part of your meals or as a delicious soup. This remedy helps eliminate kidney stones effectively.

Relief from Knee Pain:

- For knee pain relief, finely grind fenugreek seeds (methi dana) and mix one to two teaspoons of the powder with water.
- Apply this paste to the affected knee joint. Regular application, especially in old age, can alleviate knee pain. Consistent use for two to three months can yield significant results.

Enhancing Hair Shine and Luster:

- After shampooing your hair, rinse it with a glass of lukewarm water mixed with lemon juice or a few drops of vinegar.
- This simple step will leave your hair glossy, beautiful, soft, and conditioned.

Maintaining Clean Palms, Soles, and Throat:

- As advised by revered Mahatma Shri Akhilesh Ji, regularly massage your palms with oil or ghee and keep them clean.
- Similarly, maintain clean soles by applying oil or ghee and practicing regular foot care.
- The subtle connection between the palms, heart, brain, and abdomen ensures overall well-being. Keeping these areas clean contributes to a healthy heart and mind.

For Anti - Aging

- Take a spoon of coffee and mix it with a cup of water. Add 2 spoons of rice flour to the mixture.
- Now take the mixture in a saucepan and boil for 10 mins till it becomes thick in consistency.
- Pour it in a bowl, mix it well and add 1 spoon of alovera gel and 1 spoon of almond oil to it.
- The mixture is now ready to use. Apply the mixture on your face and neck, leaving it for 20 mins and finally washing it with first cold and warm water. Moisture your skin with your daily mositurizer

Naturally coloring white hair from root

- Take equal quantities of mustard oil and haldi on a flat pan. Heat the mixture on a medium flame.
- Add a packet of coffee to it and roast till it thickens. Pour the mixture out in a bowl.
- Add half a lemon alongwith a Vitamin E capsule into the mixture. Stir the contents and apply to scalp.

Cleaning Hacks

- Add hair conditioner to mopping water to prevent dust from settling on floors.
- Add white vinegar while mopping for disinfecting and removing odour.
- Combine white vinegar and toothpaste. Spray the mixture on your faucets and wipe with a clean cloth for a shiny and new look.
- Mix white vinegar and baking soda. Spray the solution over stains to wash them off easily.

Remember to consult a healthcare professional for personalized advice and treatment options. These home remedies can complement medical care but should not replace professional guidance